Floating Heart

Also by Stuart Friebert

POETRY
Dreaming of Floods
Calming Down
Up in Bed
Stories My Father Can Tell
Uncertain Health
The Darmstadt Orchids
Funeral Pie
Near Occasions of Sin
Speak Mouth to Mouth
Kein Trinkwasser
Die Prokuristen kommen
Nicht Hinauslehnen

PROSE
Der Gast, und sei er noch so schlecht: Prose Poems
The Language of the Enemy: Stories

TRANSLATIONS
Günter Eich: *Valuable Nail: Selected Poems* (with David Walker & David Young)
Karl Krolow: *On Account Of: Selected Poems*
Miroslav Holub: *Sagittal Section: Selected Poems* (with Dana Habová)
Giovanni Raboni: *The Coldest Year of Grace: Selected Poems* (with Vinio Rossi)
Marin Sorescu: *Hands Behind My Back: Selected Poems* (with Gabriela Dragnea & Adriana Varga)
Karl Krolow: *What'll We Do With This Life?: Selected Poems*
Judita Vaičiūnaitė: *Fire, Put Out By Fire: Selected Poems* (with Viktoria Skrupskelis)
Sylva Fischerová: *The Swing in the Middle of Chaos: Selected Poems* (with the author)
Karl Krolow: *Puppets in the Wind: Selected Poems*
Kuno Raeber: *Be Quiet: Selected Poems*

ANTHOLOGIES
A Field Guide to Contemporary Poetry & Poetics (with David Young; 2nd edition with David Walker & David Young)
The Longman Anthology of Contemporary American Poetry (1st & 2nd editions: with David Young)
Models of the Universe: An Anthology of the Prose Poem (with David Young)

TEXTBOOK
Max Frisch: *Als der Krieg zu Ende war*

FLOATING HEART

POEMS BY
STUART FRIEBERT

PINYON PUBLISHING
Montrose, Colorado

Copyright © 2014 by Stuart Friebert

All rights reserved. Except as permitted under the U.S. Copyright Act of 1976, no part of this publication may be reproduced, distributed, or transmitted in any form or by any means, or stored in a database or retrieval system, without the prior written permission of the publisher, except for brief quotations in articles, books, and reviews.

Cover Art by Jean Kondo Weigl

Photograph of Stuart Friebert by Sarah Friebert

Book and Cover Design by Susan E. Elliott

First Edition: April 2014

Pinyon Publishing
23847 V66 Trail, Montrose, CO 81403
www.pinyon-publishing.com

Library of Congress Control Number: 2014934146
ISBN: 978-1-936671-23-6

Acknowledgments

Thanks to the editors of the following journals, in which many of the poems originally appeared, in some instances under different titles and in slightly different versions:

AGNI, Ascent, Big Moon, Cape Rock Quarterly, Centennial Review, Chaminade Literary Review, Chariton Review, Chowder Review, Cincinnati Poetry Review, Cloudbank, Commonweal, Cube, Descant, Djinni, Embers, Gaia, Gargoyle, Great River Review, Gulf Coast, Hampden-Sydney Poetry Review, Hanging Loose, Harvard Review, Herman Review, The Journal, Michigan Quarterly Review, Mid-Atlantic Review, Mississippi Valley Review, Missouri Review, Negative Capability, New American Writing, North Dakota Review, Parnassus, Poetry Australia, Pennsylvania Review, Pittsburgh Quarterly, Pocket Pal, Poet Lore, Prairie Schooner, Prologue, Pudding, Quarterly West, Raccoon, River Oak Review, Sand Hills Review, Seattle Review, Shenandoah, Small Pond Review, Southern Poetry Review, Sou'wester, Sycamore Review, Three Rivers Journal, Treasure House, Verse, Voyages, West Branch, West Hills Review

North River Press published a limited, broadside edition of "Floating Heart."

For

D & S & S & N & K & R

Contents

I. IF WE EVER DO SEE THEM AGAIN

The Cross and the Kiss   3
Daylight Down   4
Lonesome Water   5
Lecture on Stealing   6
Quim-Quams   7
From See to Can't See   9
Water Walking Stick   10
Giraffe   11
On Yawning   12
Death Glow   13
Doctor Bird   14
Bee Catchers   15
Everglade Kite   16
Mooneye   17

II. IN THE ZENITH

Nadir   21
Spider Milkweed   22
Flatfish   24
Never is Nowadays   25
In Ancient Egypt   26
On Cradles   27
Abasicky   29

Conrad of Constance 30
Erysipeloid 31
Abraham's Tree 32
On Leaving 33
The Will 34
Destroying the Subject 35
On Getting Very Sick in a Foreign Country 37

III. NOT QUITE REMEMBERING WHAT TO DO NEXT

Samovar 41
Voltaire 42
Pink of the Evening 43
Holiday 44
Rembrandt's Missing Pope 45
Nuns Fishing 46
Adam and Eve (1504) 48
Zaunkönig 50
Ruach/Rauch 51
Leaving the Museum 53
Hark 54
Zitronencreme 56

IV. TRUSTWORTHY LEGEND?

Back of Beyond 61
The Tornado Month 62
Floating Heart 64

Dock Spider   65
Winter Flounder   67
Quarter Horse Curse   68
Christmas Dinner   69
On Panking   70
These Arguments   72
Beazlestone   73
Rabbit Dew   74

V. ALMOST AN AFTERTHOUGHT

On Love   77
Knautschke   78
Blacknose Shark   79
The Tanks   80
Near Dachau   81
More on Lying   82
Einstein in Berlin   83
Somewhere Near Minsk   84
Honorable Intentions   86
But That the Wicked Turn   87
Shadow   88
Anadromous   89
Moonlight's   90
Hooked Deep   91
Shoes   93
Admitting We Were Born   94
Thank the One Above   95
On the Eve of the End   101

I. IF WE EVER DO SEE THEM AGAIN

THE CROSS AND THE KISS

Remember when we couldn't read or write?
Just make a cross, right here, someone said,
related to the king. Now kiss it the way
you would your Gramma's Bible, so we know
you're behind us all the way. He left and we
went back to our awkward gestures of love.

These days, the steady thunder of our pens
and pencils would make our ancestors think
of mountains falling down. When I kiss you
I want intimacy; but for now, separate as
we are, these little *xxxes*, curiously still,
will have to do instead. They reach your
eyes, which, under their black lashes, keep
my cry in the darkness alive, and nothing
else of your face can be seen for tears.

DAYLIGHT DOWN

The old-fashioned end of the day's light,
when the dark comes right after sunset;
dark as Egypt, say, voices lower, as if
from very far away. We open the door,
and head out into the yard, hope to take
a long-exposure photo of the sole blooming
poppy at lot's edge, which always arrives
for our daughter's birthday. Resident rabbit
is out there, too, still as a saucer. I would,
excuse me for saying so, I would like to
taste—its meat. Oh my, it *is* delicious!
you say, Unless of course we really eat it;
but someone's forgotten the proper wine,
and there's a baby underfoot, rosy-cheeked.

LONESOME WATER

Drink it and back you go, sometimes
as far as your childhood home, to die.
Gravels clear it, willows dapple it, while
your thoughts turn to changes for the worse.

It's more and more possible for your
parents to bring evidence against you.
They dance around your bed, pull at
your flesh, crack nasty jokes in a state
of near frenzy. Will it be over soon,

you ask, your voice running down,
your fever spiking. Maybe they are
in love with you in their own fashion,
maybe they're merely saving you from
terrible secrets, you think at last, while

out in the woods, the stream's filling
with water again after years of drought.

LECTURE ON STEALING

After I think I've finished,
her eyelids flutter. She thinks,
Here he goes again ... I see her
make a fist as if I were taking
her blood pressure. She pushes
back a cry. Quick, how'll I ease
her out again, she's under my nail.

I light a match, keep the needle in
till it chars: a father going after
a sliver, protecting a little body
above the wrist. There, it's out!
Go and cross yourself three times.

She moves past the little table
near her bed, kicks one shoe off,
picks up a foot to look: Daddy,
there's another sliver, here!

Old wooden serpent sliding again.

QUIM-QUAMS

What my dad said I had if I seemed
upset in the slightest. "I'm really not,"
I'd protest. I'd just get the wobbles,

had to lie down when I did. I admit
I didn't take my shirt or shoes off,
hit the brandy bottle if they persisted,

till the words surged to my lips, "Don't fret,
we'll get along some day, Dad, just wait."
He's oiling his twelve-gauge again, which

I'm supposed to inherit, but he's given up
showing me how to take it apart, put it back
together, so if I'm ever drafted he says I'd

have a leg up. Sometimes it seems life's
whole meaning can be summed up in his
one zinger: PROVE IT, which'd mean

myself to him. When I finally learned to
lead the duck till its half-crazed smile froze
on its face, the shell hit home. Dad led me

by the neck to where it lay. I tried resisting.
Knives and forks, not to mention weapons,
would have had to be invented first. All

this had to happen so many times before I
could breathe without a paper sack and Dad
no longer had to tilt my head back, no longer

looked me in the eye, no longer stroked my feverish temples with his stocky fingers.

FROM SEE TO CAN'T SEE

It's the darkness before sunrise,
or after sunset. Time to look down,

pat your hound's head. No, no, no, boy.
We're not chasing another fat rabbit.

Could anything be more vexing than
having to go on when you can't see?

I can't go on, I'll go on, Beckett
said somewhere, so I shift my eyes

higher. In time there'll be stars.
But for now it's darker than hiding

your face in your hands, gunny-sacking
everything; your body quivering, the dog

shivering, while those particles
the physicists believe in roll right

through you. I'm ready for another
Big Bang; little it-bits of blackness

beginning to learn to be lightning.
I pull my face slowly out of my hands.

WATER WALKING STICK

> —on Darwin's daughter
> just having died …

Looking for all the world like a dried twig,
it climbs among the weeds along pond margins;
so perfectly camouflaged it has few enemies.

Watching it, ideas one once had that were fat
grow lean, while the insect petrifies, waiting
for one to make the next move. It has been two

hours of locked-in, mutual silence by his watch,
when the stick seems to twitch a bit, or at least
the lily pad underfoot takes on an extra drop of

water that pools around it. Normally, he can't
keep still in any place, wanders around restless,
sometimes quite unhappy, his tongue lisping

inanities; at other times so beaten by such sticks
he runs for a cliff and jumps off; into a river
dream, or he wouldn't be crouching down now

to see if his eyes can make out its eyes. There
they are! Little black pin cushions at the bends
in, what, its legs? With every blink he sinks

deeper into the dark well of something other,
which will come to grief in its own way, though
the rest of us he hoped would try to stay happy.

GIRAFFE

A neck of only seven bones, like the lowly mouse.
Legs all the same length, even though you'd swear

the hind ones are shorter. Keen smell and sight
(beautiful eyes!). Can outrun most predators but

once overtaken, is easily killed, alas. Quite a piece
of work, all in all; but can you imagine having no

voice, not being able to utter the slightest sound,
even in extreme danger? Numbed by fear, even

a child can cry. Rearing, plunging, backing, side-
stepping, a few last flings before planting all

four hooves to brace for the lion's last lunge.
Watching from afar, our hearts sink, but our

screams rise; and we look down to drown our
sorrow, while the giraffe swallows its tongue.

ON YAWNING

After you start to, just try to stop. Oh,
you can close your mouth, but some
muscles go on contracting. See me yawn,
you will too, as we know. All this ought
to be clearer, but scientists still can't
say for certain it's the hypothalamus
behind it all. And I'm not sure that
Shakespeare's not on the right track:
*When graveyards yawn, and graves give
up their dead ...* Something like that.

When the funeral director realized
mother was lowered into the wrong
grave, he waved his arms wildly and
hollered, For God's sake, winch her
right back up! Need I add the winch
jammed, and there she sat, and there
we sat, till Dad leaned forward on
his walker, then hollered right back,
You know what your mother would say,
don't you? For cripesake, Ed, I told
you to read the damn instructions ...
Then Dad yawned so hard it shook his
head like a puppet, and he nodded off
halfway through the boring service.

DEATH GLOW

It's winter but there's thunder.
Dad's doctor knocks and enters
before I can say, Yes? He goes
to draw the drapes, when I stop
him: Can't you please give Dad
more morphine? It can't be long
now, and he's struggling. Don't
worry, we won't accuse you of
addicting him. Doc's not amused,
and motioning to the nurse steps
into the hall. I hear them argue.

When I go to moisten Dad's lips,
his eyes brighten, cheeks flush;
and for a moment I think, he'll
pull through, but of course he
doesn't. That rattle comes along
between short phrases, long pauses,
and the constant turn of his head.
I fall asleep. He's dead when I wake.

DOCTOR BIRD

In the swamps down here, it's the one
with the huge bill. The guides who go
way back under the densest branches
sometimes call it Doctor Jesus, who
comes when one's way past recovery.

If we ever do see them again, we try
to avoid their eyes – we weren't put
here for such knowledge, sinful in
its essence, fed out of a bottle as
an infant, or better yet, a rosy nipple.

We feel tired at the right time, fall
asleep like an airplane entering
a thick cloud. Whatever people try
to make out then, we're high and dry,
long before they've scanned the sky.

So high all that's left is a witness
pointing up, It's a bird, a plane, no …
It's Doctor Bird, consulting with
Doctor Jesus, and faith, not logic
now, obtains, going in and out;
in and out among us, under cover.

BEE CATCHERS

Or robber flies, in these parts;
can carry insects far heavier than
themselves, but the year's drawing

to an end now. I must conquer this
melancholy if I can. Nabokov might
have pinned their bodies neatly onto

coarse paper for winter study, or
suspended them in liquid, looking
like lumps of dough. He'd look

for bubbles rising to the surface,
a clue to what was going on inside.
It's said he worked harder over them

than words, without so much as a head-
ache, powdering and painting even the
commonest varieties. I put some soup

on for lunch, wish I could ask him over,
but in human form. After coffee I'd bring
out all the tiny bodies the bee catchers

have dropped my way, flying by in July;
beg him to read them, draw the blood off
my brain so I could drift. In the dream

words tell the truth like insects, won't let
themselves be made into anything else.

EVERGLADE KITE

There are only one or two spots in the country
where with luck you can see one, and one's right
near my mother's grave down south. Past the tiny,
blue-gray body, drawn with fearful accuracy, look
for that sleek, much-hooked bill. Its thrifty old ways
continue, make me miss her wooden crutches. She had
been rather vain for her winged accomplishments;
kept sitting in the corner doing crosswords, waving
for more nectar. I cleaned her glasses with a bow,
while drifting over the rocks in the tide, digging
in the garden for more than worms. Even the moon
took on an anxious look. I'd started telling her not
to worry. I was where I was, doing what I'd done;
and wouldn't leave her till she forgave me, when
we caught sight of the kite. The reel went slack;
she looked down at me, stopped mid-air. Can't you
let me have my death, she chirped. I cut the string.

MOONEYE

I try to catch one once a year.
Off the dock's the best place.

It's not quite a herring; flesh
drier, even fuller of small bones.

So we really never eat it, just
take in those eyes. Otherwise,

it's quite ugly. You cry when
I urge you to touch one. It's

too abstract, you say, I can't.
Before releasing it, I hold it up

to the moon, which winks back.

II. IN THE ZENITH

NADIR

In the book I'm reading—instead of painting
the fence so father will holler again when he
comes home—it's the point in space directly
below which I'm lying in the hammock,
looking up, the sky a half-dome whose edges
form a great circle that rests on the surface.
Drop a plumb line, the book suggests, and
it will pass through the center of the earth;
and back out into space again, as far as
the center of the half-dome below.

We're in the zenith then. If you keep looking
up and down, snapping your head like that,
mother said, Your teeth will turn black and
fall out; besides, if we do our duty, God takes
good care of us. Now pry that paint can open,
make that brush fly. I don't want another of
your father's fits. It's late, and growing up
on the Steppes of Russia, we never showed
ourselves till the sky was bedaubed with light.
Nobody knew from nadir or zenith, my young
astronomer, but we knew from right and wrong.
Now get that job done before your father yells,
so we can have some real peace in this house.

SPIDER MILKWEED

White flowers, thin leaves; nondescript, yet a.k.a.
immortal, for its curative powers, I read. Mother

strained it and I drank it for my first serious catarrh
before all the –cillins and –mycins came along, so

father stopped grinding up powders with his mortar
and pestle, sold the pharmacy for a song. Looking

back, maybe I was just tired and thirsty, used to cross
myself in secret, wanted to die a Christian like Georgie,

true son of the sweet Greek family across the street,
who scooped my cat Snookie up when she was run over

by a streetcar on 35th & Meinecke, and veiled in tears
brought her to our door. I wailed till mother led me back

to bed. "She has other thoughts of the matter," father said
when he came home late after another slow day. "Now don't

forget to water this little spider, I'll set it on the sill. I wish
I could sit up with you till it blooms." Mother's voice gruffed

as if she were about to hit him. I've thought about my parents'
marriage ever since. When someone asked mother at their 50th

if she'd do it all over again, "Enough of your cleverness" is
all she'd say. When I persisted, she sighed, "You're stupid

but not pious, at least there's that." I bundled her into the car for the icy ride home on the dark freeway. Wintry evenings are

ever more frightening. Sure, the milkweed's hibernating now, but soon its spiders will emerge again. Bite me hard, I'll beg!

FLATFISH

The ancient ones, having had to
get way down in size to make it
through the crevices and slots.
They're just about as rare as
worn, narrow stairs; the ones
my mother's climbing to bring
me supper—a flounder's good at
the beginning of convalescence,
although those eyes still frighten
me, as if someone had just given
the creature a beating. I steal
a look back at the bay my father
caught it in, and life turns into
a moment, and a thousand years
at once; the way it can when God
asks how you've learned to live yours.
Just a mistake, you say, The priest
gave me a Bible, saying "Nothing
in this world is without a choice,
so pray eat up what your poor father
has caught, and your poor mother
fried in the fat of this nice fire."

NEVER IS NOWADAYS

The fiddler's preparing his fiddle.
If there were clouds, they'd be beautiful
potato clouds. The bride's fumbling with
her buttons. Uncle's spread out on the bed,
lighting cigarettes end to end. If Aunt were
still alive, she'd be singing a dirty song.

Sitting back against a miserable tree, I'm
the groom of course, and I'll marry her
I suppose. I'm not Hungarian for nothing,
and never is nowadays. Pretty soon music
starts up. We're waiting for the priest who's
paddling ashore toward the lights on the dock.

Don't stand up, Father, someone shouts, You
know you can't swim! Does a deaf man come
late? he yells. It's later now, can you tell I'm
getting frightened; I'm within a hair of going
along with everything. Does anyone know
what God was like in the time of Christ?

IN ANCIENT EGYPT

After scaling cliffs, jumping ditches,
sometimes running for their life toward
the fields, families too poor to afford
meat, I read, made cakes in the shape
of pigs. It was not a life with lamps
hanging from the ceiling. In short,

they were tormented, no peace day or
night, hallucinations rife. Sometimes,
things seem no better now; so many
humans all over the globe, looking
after their pigs as they would a child;
raising their voices when they'd rather

lower them in the claustrophobic museum;
stammering when their bellies are pointed to.
My own children point to the exhibit under
glass: Yes, yes, we can learn a great deal
from the ancients, I say so loudly the guard
wakes up, tear my heart out, throw it on
the floor, stomp on it, whisper in their ear
when I finally calm down: We're richer
than we were last year, and the year before.

ON CRADLES

—for Betsy

Earliest ones, we're told, were hewn
from half logs that swayed and rolled,
baby tied down with dark leather thongs,
rocked by Mama's foot, who sat working
and humming wild, first lullabies; pine
cones, twigs and cones tucked in as toys.

Moses, as any standard Bible will tell you,
had something of a papyrus basket plastered
with bitumen and pitch that didn't have to
double as a tiny boat, luckily. Who knows
what the Nile would have cast against it?

Anthropologists say first Laplanders swung
their babes in hammocks lined with seal fur.
Fastening them to walrus tusks, they stuck
them into their huts' icy walls and clapped
till the wind went just right; and sleep could
come to all, the reindeer crowding in about.

From the picture of Henry VIII's, you can see
why he'd eventually go crazy over some things:
the little contraption had a hooded cowl that
could be raised for sun and smiles, lowered
for cries and scowls. A different model, who
knows, Anne might have lived a normal life.

Friends in Florence have had one in the family
since 1713. Their daughter dons a Communion
frock to rock her dolly in it, while I read her
favorite Bible stories and stare hard at I.H.S.
carved deeply into the headboard. Christ is
a new experience for me at this low level.

Prosperous early Americans covered theirs
with several leathers, and intricate patterns
of brass nails. Ben Franklin's said to have
tried a cleaner design, but turned to lightning
instead, while Tom Paine fed his to the fire
in one of those awful winters fit for no man.

Our son in Zurich in the Sixties, having been
scolded on the playground for sticking a finger
into the fountain—That's for birds, someone's
nanny shrieked—climbed into his sister's and
bunged his mouth with thumb. We used little
knobs on the outside to tie him safely inside.

But the one out the window today, of fine grass,
with gray lichens, lined with milkweed floss, is
clearly a hummingbird's, not trusting to others.

ABASICKY

What you do when you yell, Shame on you!
In that children's game, namely move an index
finger of one hand along at right angles to
the index finger of the other; in my direction,
for what I've just done—thumped you with
my crutch, it seems. Not hard, mind you,
because I've not got much strength to spare,
just enough to discourage you from pitying me
in such a state. Oh, I can learn a foreign tongue,
I can wind my watch, I can sip my juice through
a straw; very slowly I admit. Would you come
next Sunday too, please? We'll make a party
of it; I'm sorry I lashed out at you, who were
just admiring the tea set the lovely nurses use
on this ward, where legs are mainly two bits
of wood; and the owl the children bring, made
from a clothes pin with round eyes drawn in
at the end. Look closer, the face is all mine.

CONRAD OF CONSTANCE

We see him almost always with a chalice & a spider,
because, celebrating Mass back way back when, one

silked down into it. Though all were thought to be
poisonous, that one really was, so swallowing it,

out of respect for the Eucharist, he died. "Come and
have a cup with us," his way of inviting his flock to

partake of the mysteries, is what my mother said when
she began her nightly drinking. For me it was hot milk,

because to the end she wouldn't corrupt me, and I drank
heartily from a cup incised with a bitty spider her mother

saved from a hard white Russian childhood, which I'll soon
pass on to Kazu Conrad, our grandson, middle-named after

my wife's good father. If he cries, may it only be over spilt
milk, tenderly trap even a black widow that makes it inside,

even as far as his pillow, for if there's no mercy there's no
decency either. He's a dear boy who likely won't preside

over Mass, but when he sings to himself, watching the spider
touch its way down the stoop, we find happiness watching, too.

ERYSIPELOID

An infection that often starts when a fish bone
punctures your finger. Swelling and a purplish
red discoloration soon set in, spread to your hand
and on down to the tip of the adjoining finger.

Blood poisoning set in the last time it happened,
so this time I dropped everything and headed for
the clinic in Nonesuch, near the Kentucky lake
I'd been cleaning out, catching way too many

spawning bass defending their nests, sometimes
the same one over and over for the stupid thrill
of hauling in a whopper, when it finally hit me:
Enough already, my father would say, How much

can a reasonable man eat, anyway? The last time
we fished together, the sky beginning to pale in
the late afternoon light, I'd been tempted to disagree.
We were good at spending whole days arguing, then;

looking at each other with a peculiar impatience,
mother beseeching us to grow up. She almost left.
Forty years of fishing together, not finding happiness,
but now that he's gone I'm frightened, can't find it

on my own. Easing the hook out as gently as possible,
cradling the bass in my cold hands, I was just about to
slip it back into the lake when it suddenly twisted. After
a shot, "Better leave the wound open," the doctor said.

ABRAHAM'S TREE

No leaves, nothing to climb. I mean those long
feathers and plumes of cirrus clouds radiating
from a single point on the horizon. I used to
stick a patch on one eye to draw them better
with the other, the Old Testament fading fast
at my feet. Friends point a finger, You ought
to get back to your origins; and I can't deny
the guilt, like too much fat in chicken soup,
come to gag you. When I ask you, a Christian,
who knows what came before Abraham, and
what after, you say Hebrew's not hard to learn.
You just sound it out, like picking money off
the floor. But you didn't quit Hebrew School
to have a chance at playing shortstop. Grampa
went on one of his limited hunger strikes. "Oy,
he said, "He has never learned the difference
between our Abe and Lincoln, draws nothing
but Civil War cannon all the time." Which I
don't deny; but then I hadn't fallen in love
with you yet—risking marrying a blond shiksa,
who's a great favorite with God, who believes
in the journey to self-perfection; which leads
to trees, never clouds; who has always lent
a hand to this poor soul, just now beginning
to get a foot up over the lowest branches.

ON LEAVING

What do you mean you're through with the fence,
Dad said. The creosote's got to go around the posts
between coats, bet you forgot. I assure you you're
not the first to whom a son has promised more than
he's delivered, my mother's mirror added. You never
pushed me high enough, sis would whine; though he
was only five, my brother banged his golf club on
the cart for one more round. The cat couldn't talk,
but it was written all over her whiskers: I swear
you love me less than the dog, where's my Fancy
Treat? I don't understand, my uncle said, You used
to be able to lift me in my wheelchair. Aunt Polly
began to empty her chamber pot herself. Cousins
Jan and June, twins, stopped offering me their tiny
nipples underwater at the lake. The cop at the cross
walk began checking my license. Still, it wasn't till
Grampa Joe died of lead poisoning from painting all
the houses in town summers (he was the high school
principal) that I knocked on every door, tipped my cap:
I'll be going now, so long everybody, and don't worry.

THE WILL

My mother in her armchair looked
into the fire. My father had taken
his position near the door. Once,
he began to mumble something. I
thought I knew what to do for them,
put on some soothing music, but
they began to cry. Very well, I said,
We'll go to the drawer with the will,
see who gets what. It'll shorten things.

There's no such will, mother said,
and father nodded. It looked for
a moment as if matters had always
gone well, no one hurrying up from
somewhere; there was little wealth,
but enough gaiety; and we were
never done with our food. Standing
in our socks, starting some old joke.
Life being different from death; hoping
we might go on and on and on and on.

DESTROYING THE SUBJECT

Undressing;
waiting on the body;
the fault's not mine yet;
back molars don't matter
anymore. The feeling is
of being shoved into
a leather bag: mad,
foolish; get a cane
for Christmas.

Smelling the body
with some astonishment;
walking to the back bathroom,
the groin a plot where mirrors
no longer grow. Flowers,
Europe in January, Tebaldi
at La Scala, her new year
full of rage; my hands
full of reasons, the usher
rushing backstage with
my program: is she doing
me a kindness by signing it?

Asleep on Lufthansa now;
should be home in a few years,
dropping one skin, wrapping
myself in another. After
the goose, they make
a plaster cast of the lower
half of my body, tuck it under
the rosebush by the garage.

There are two of me again.
I sleepwalk back to the house,
moonlight pickling my shoulders.

ON GETTING VERY SICK IN A FOREIGN COUNTRY AND BEATING IT THE HELL HOME

1 *Trying to remember the painting you loved,
  you fall down the museum steps, break a leg*

She who was once the helmet maker's beautiful wife
is now your nurse. Strip to your socks and shoes,
she says. Put this on, it ties in back. We'll give
you something to put you half to sleep, something
to dry your mouth; you allergic to anything at all?
No, no, I like them all, you cry, lie down on a cot,
behave yourself, get rolled into a tiny dark office.
A doctor dressed in a naval uniform shakes your
hand, while cleaning his ears with a dirty Q-tip.

2 *Town square: people and cars milling around*

Like going for a ride in the dark: just as you recall
you've eaten something that's disagreed with you,
a black Citroën stops; and a man inside hands you
a bunch of radishes. You tear one off, pop it in your
mouth: suddenly, there's pain; you forget how to swim,
lose hold of the lifeline, fall off the raft, try to wave.

3 *Dusty room at night*

The baby in the basket's gone! the woman beside you
cries. Just a woman on a burro. Get a woman on a burro
in mind, your conscience always says; hope the burro's not
on top. Any woman, holding a child's hand, a bundle on

her scarfed head. But it should be a woman coming out
a pink door, you think, waiting for a bus with a gold star
on its side; one from Here to There: please not too many
stitches, Captain Doctor of the Clean Ears! And please,
a receipt so I can collect on my miserable insurance.

4 *Hysteria sets in*

I have diarrhea, trouble breathing, sleeping; a pin of a pain
in my chest. My back, my foot hurt; I'm constipated, but,
more than anything, can you direct me to a pawnshop please?
Are all my meals included? I don't know how to use this.
Please speak more slowly; something's the matter with
my head. Excuse me, what time is it, officer? You sure?

5 *Reading Kafka on the train to Prague*

He smiles. He doesn't seem to give a damn.
Oh, I can see I can't stop him, which I regret.
I like my Swiss watch, it's so expensive; but
I just don't trust it, and go before a magistrate.
Judge, what time is it, please? Time to go now?

6 *Back home*

A nice family in a small town on the Ohio River.
A comfortable old red brick house that just needs
a little work; on the gutters, the bricks, you name it,
buddy. Oh, and a clever way to keep the pigeons off.
And a rusty old car in the driveway, so I can climb in
the back seat, close the windows before lightning strikes.

III. NOT QUITE REMEMBERING WHAT TO DO NEXT

SAMOVAR

From Indo-European *awe*, to moisten or to flow,
whence water. The one in our family, from Poland,
ca. 1745, is the usual urn with a tarnished spigot.

Once, I took it apart to see what made it tick; but
there was no internal tubing for heating the water,
which the encyclopedia depicted, just a little hill
of ashes; from whence, Gramma said when I asked,
all our ancestors flowed, blessings or no. Even her
sin-child with Feodor; him of one name only, whose
picture she carried around her stout neck like a noose,
and lightly kissed when she sipped tea from her glass,
through the sugar cube she clenched between her teeth.

VOLTAIRE

>—for David

Had red hair, which may explain why
he called Shakespeare a barbarian,
with a hole in his soul. Left to him,
we'd still not know if Othello ever
strangled Desdemona. The crucial day,
when Voltaire could have ruled either
way, he ordered carrots and white wine.
The sun was burning behind a thin veil
of clouds. He tried to read a little more,
the chaos of Shakespeare's sounds whirling
through the garden, which was soon made
narrow as a ditch, and Iago came running
toward him, covered with sores, his hair
falling away everywhere, like decaying
plaster; and so perhaps we can understand
Voltaire bending down to pick up a stone,
the words still flying at him off Iago's
lips, and his heart jumping as he realized
these characters would always be strangers,
speaking in unfettered rhythms; and throwing
the stone, Voltaire was heard to shout, nay
scream, Not on my beloved Paris stage!

PINK OF THE EVENING

"Pink is as pink supposes," said
Gertrude Stein one late afternoon,
just before dusk. In France, of course,
with Mr. Hemingway coming over for
something to drink, work to show,
advice to get, but we can't be sure.

"I will tell you YES. YES yes yes yes.
Yes AH yesssss, most certainly YESSS!
Mr. Hemingway," I imagine her saying;
"And I will tell you NOOO, oh my Lord
NO," maybe even "NOPE, nosireeesir, No!
And then you must go home to figure out
the difference," is what I hope she finally
offered to do for him, more or less …

Some birds came along over drinks, and
Alice may have said, "It's too early for
the ravens; they're sure to be waxwings."
"Who cares?" Gertrude would sigh, "As
long as Mr. Hemingway won't shoot them."

The sky dark, the last raven, petrified,
let the end of its pink ribbon slip to its
breast, then tugged hard to noose its neck.

HOLIDAY

A spot missed by a painter's brush,
the special dictionary says; except
for Rembrandt, who left none; scythed
around the edges of stones; brushed
every feather clean on hats; dusted
pears and apples in their heavy bowls;
but all the rest take one now and then,
and no wonder. They're human, get tired,
step back, rub an eye; but not Rembrandt.
Even after his own figure foreshortened
and shadowed, he kept right on painting
as if glued to the canvas, the brush sort of
in the way. No, it is not all right, he said,
when friends pulled his sleeve to go out
for a stein of beer around the corner. I'll
imbibe later, he'd say, Only an ass would
stop now! Then he'd laugh, that dark face
coming back, old friend in the oval mirror.

REMBRANDT'S MISSING POPE

The sharp eye of the owl,
now that's a blessed thing.

And all these nuns around,
stern unto themselves, are

nonetheless kind to us,
wouldn't you say, van Rijn?

There, I've pricked you
on the tongue. I think

the Pope said to put
a little earth on it, or

it will flicker in and out;
inferiors dismiss superiors;

and genius on this occasion
is conquered by calculation.

NUNS FISHING

—for Barbara

For what, may I ask, when I pass by
along the shore of the shallow bay,

careful to seem politely nonchalant,
not to stare at the little black crosses

nestled against their soft white robes,
their faces as one in the setting sun.

Without taking her eye off her bobber,
one says with something of a lisp, Just

the John Dory, the one with that black
spot Saint Peter's thumbprint left when

he took a coin from its mouth. God save us
from His secrets, I try, the only words I find,

which prompts her to put down her pole,
slowly approach me, a fixed, heavy look

in her black eyes. I thought you weren't
coming, she says at last, as if I'd been

expected for years. Yes, well, here I am,
go on please, I say, as if looking at a view

of a huge storm in her album, the moon
burning behind a veil of unbroken clouds.

Suddenly, the other nuns reel in their lines,
leave the two of us standing there, breathing

the air between us. My fishing years are past,
I finally manage to say. Yes, yes, I know, she

nods, It's like being without sunlight when
Father's away, but it's not for me to say how
to live on. She takes up her pole again, while
I draw circles in the sand, her tears in my eyes.

ADAM AND EVE (1504)

Stop gazing at the humans, start looking
for the animals edging the etching, mother
said to teach me the four humours, which
broke free once the apple was eaten.

Choleric

According to medieval sages, witches talked
with cats, both of which were burned together:
Look Dürer's in the eye: even on cloudy days
the pupils slit when the sun's overhead. Omit
its next meal if the tongue's coated, administer
mineral oil instead: a well cat catches more mice.

Melancholic

That's the elk, whose coat's mostly brown, rump
yellow, but Dürer left his colors in the shed where
he'd go to mope. A big bull keeps a harem of
at least a dozen females: calves come in May
or June, one to a cow, usually. Many will die of
starvation or predation if wolves abound; grounds
for dismal thoughts in dreams growing darker.

Phlegmatic

The ox of course, said to have first come from
the Old World. Heavy of body, long of tail, split
hooves and horns smooth and curved; but a heavy
yoke will slow most temperaments. Thanks be to
their rich milk, satisfying meat and soft leather.

Sanguine

Cut up for stew, the rabbit gives its blood almost cheerfully, Dürer's mother observed. Her son said he'd be home for supper with quite an appetite after stowing his graver. It was near the end of his life.

ZAUNKÖNIG

What the Germans called a new torpedo in
their arsenal, "fitted with a listening device

so it homed onto sounds of ships' propellers."
The Brits called it "gnat," and there you have

the difference in their minds: German for "wren,"
the perfect English word for the tough little bird,

while "Zaun" ("fence") and "König" ("king"),
as you can see, aside from ignoring many other

birds that light on fences, goes poetical to put it
badly, which reminds me of Mozartian melodies

German pilots listened to on London bombing runs.
When I listen to Amadeus these days, I pull my cap

over my ears with both hands, clamber into the little
cockpit of our car, and go off in no hurry toward town.

Not a wren in sight on the fences, some of which need
new slats and paint. Now and then a red-tailed hawk

drops down out of the drowsy sky with something to eat
wriggling in its talons. Politely, it turns its back to dig in,

shows me a yawn as if to say, See, nice and clean now, no
rubble below, and soon takes flight again, growing smaller.

RUACH/RAUCH

—for Amy

This is not an eye test. Please relax.
Ruach may then come upon you, even

enter your nostrils – see Job; eventually
allow you to speak, act on behalf of God:

divinely inspired, wind of inspiration to
others, morphing at certain moments into

rayach nichoach, a pleasing scent: how
burning sacrifices smell to the Lord. Not

that certain odor from some 20th century
chimneys, borne aloft by *Rauch = smoke*

in English, though I was also taught in
beginning German is cognate with *ruach*:

"Just feel your mouth fill with your breath
when you say it properly," Mr. Staub said,

who we thought was a refugee until he wasn't.
I wrote him years later after a philology class:

Sir, *Rauch* is from Anglo-Saxon *rok*; Germanic:
Rauki, Low Dutch *rook*. "Ah, how nice to think

of the blackest of birds, too. Folk etymologists
would have a field day, now wouldn't they?" He

died before we could exchange many more post-
cards, but one I still have from Auschwitz reads,

"Such nice scenery, wish you were here." At first
I ran off to the woods, climbed some branches till

night came on, the stars misting around the moon,
my head going round, and I found myself past all

shameful thoughts, ready to open my old Beginning
Hebrew text again, which I'd tossed aside when sweet
Rabbi Stein warned me against studying anything but.

LEAVING THE MUSEUM

We were nice to all the artists.
Didn't judge, just admired, walked
right up to their work—the guards
got nervous!—shook our heads just
so, stepped back amazed, held hands.

What was your favorite detail? Mine
you know, because I know you were
bored—I went back a hundred times—
was the parakeet the Jesus child was
holding in Jacopo di Cione's triptych:

I admit I reduce everything to a tiny
moment, while you think more wholly.
Snow's stopped, see? And our lips work
with no desire to speak. I don't often cry,
but you make tears come to my eyes.
Thoughts of the future seem improper.

My eyes can't get going again. You take
my hand, pull me toward the last bus.
In the darkness, trying to glimpse you
in the glass, taking in other words that
helpless middle way, in the darkness,
in the bus, in your image, which I touch …

HARK

Or "Horch" in German. Also you may remember
the old name of that fabled open car Hitler drove
into our bones till the company Latinized it to Audi

after the war. In the faded, blurry photo before me
Kennedy's head suddenly superimposes itself over
Hitler's rigid body, one of those mind's eye's tricks

guaranteed to induce periodic insomnia. Where was
Oswald back then: there were many windows in attics
no one hung out of to wave, throw flowers or shout.

Everything below was worn, covered with stains, even
robbing AH of some self-respect. Before Eva's chaste
hands twinned around his neck, he forgot himself for

an instant till the bile boiled up again. In later pics he
stands up now and then, wagging his tongue with more
muscle. "They must be taught a lesson," she said he'd

say over and over, so he gave them one, then another,
and another; till a decade later they were caught in that
bunker, having *Malzkaffee* and heels of moldy bread;

while Russian troops were removing things from shelves,
putting them to each other's ears, talking animatedly till
sleeping it off and no one would say in the wildest dream,

"Ich bin ein Berliner." I'm beginning to tell my grandson
about some of it now, starting with the stubble on the faces
of the soldiers kicking the ground around the bunker. He

tries to listen but his eyes droop, his mouth opens slowly
and we both start yawning. "Tell me about it another time,"
he finally manages to interrupt. I nod, look for his blanket.

He can manage buckling himself now into the Audi's seat
for the ride back to his house. There's more tenderness in
his heart than in mine. Who can forget the way he looks

at you when you look at him a little too much? I should
have nothing to complain of anymore, resolve to show him
more pictures of lambs and ewes, fields of yellow flowers.

ZITRONENCREME

—for Sylva

The lemon mousse after the Christmas goose:
back in 1933 it was, when after baptized Jews

blew out the candles on the tree and led their
children to the Christmas Eve supper, servants

left behind to pitch the bucket of water at any
wayward candle, blessings were said and hopes

were high "the storm" would blow over, but of
course it wouldn't & didn't. Grampa would talk

and talk till Gramma flew at him and seized him
by the sleeve. Shortly afterward, when uncle Julius

disappeared, even the children realized they'd best
pull their caps down farther over their brows, not

repeat a word of talk around the house. "Lord, how
afraid they must have been," my mother took to

saying when she sliced up the brisket for Sunday
meals in Milwaukee in the weeks after the war.

From time to time I've asked myself if heavy hugs
and kisses had kept most of the family from fleeing

Senice, even after great gramma Fanny was murdered
at the age of 102: in the album, she's wiping her hands

on her apron before she walks out into the flock of SS in the yard, pecking away at the icing on the mousse.

IV. TRUSTWORTHY LEGEND?

BACK OF BEYOND

In the middle of nowhere, way back
of most everywhere you've been (it's
tempting to add, only God knows where),

there's likely to be a little bell, ring it
so the country doctor's buggy will stop
at the gate. Afterward, after whatever

he does to you, after he closes his little
black bag, you drink to the end of night.
Looking back now, through the snowflakes,

the sky's not as it should be, and a cold wind
pushes you into a corner, your fists clenching.
Sleep won't come, not even the tiniest wink.

THE TORNADO MONTH

It is April and lonely; we
have no idea how April, how
lonely. In exile, in Zurich,
the feeling is of watching
some dead king float among
the swans. We snap a picture
and feed them in gratitude.
We are not the kind of humans
who go after the great birds.
There are masses for him, but
we only hear the massive clocks.

We knew the taste once; now,
there is not enough time for
grace to intervene like some
obscene thing we had pulled
from our open mouth. We see
wrong things about beauty in
our grizzly madness. How can
we separate life from our life?

It started with a road, always
the dust, running thickly uphill
into a small town, with some men
talking in trees or bedrooms
to the dark red blossoms.

The bullet made the neck feverish,
the cheek ungainly, forced the hazel
eye straight down on the slow
alphabet of heroes …

Is this dying in old relation
to God, or the newness of it
just filled with trustworthy legend?

The temptation to disturb others with death
hangs framed in three colors above the bed;
a quaint text, a painted text, a forgery.

Which moon struck rays
in the strange branches of his eyes?
Now he lies, the wide split in his legs,
which did not carry him over.

The light will turn shoot-green
in another tornado month of April.

FLOATING HEART

Loves a shallow pond, spreads
its tiny white flowers over broad

leaves; and proceeds till it covers
the whole surface, sometimes in just

one summer. If you're foolish enough
to turn it over, look for the heart,

legend has it you'll not only not
catch the pickerel lurking underneath,

you'll quarrel with those you love,
cry yourself to sleep with worry; and

in the morning head nude and cold for
the old rowboat, tied to a stump; climb

aboard, paddle quickly out to the middle,
then float back slowly ashore in a wooden

coffin, when the pickerel goes belly up.

DOCK SPIDER

She's hung her egg sac in the corner of
the tire bumper at the end of the dock.

By the time I tie up after a hard day's
fishing, I see she's down a leg already.

Who knows where it ended up? But she uses
the other seven, elaborate ebony chopsticks,

to fork water striders skimming the lake's
surface right under her web. She's stretched

out so flat and black you can't see her for
the tire at first, but oh how you gasp when

I pull you down on a knee to point her out!
I'm not about to pretend I'm not horror-struck

as well: she'd be a match for a baby octopus.
Chris, the dockhand, who knows these things,

says she's on the way to dying, having done
her job; and will soon position herself so that

her hatching babies won't miss their first
meal, by which time she'll be liquefying.

I mumble something about mother's milk, but
you say she should be called the Jesus spider.

For days we force ourselves to follow nature's
little drama, as the egg sac quivers, and she

barely moves an inch away, ignoring anything
her web traps. On our last night, gunning back

before a sudden storm, scrambling to secure
the canoe, we almost forget to have a look,

when you pull me down beside you. At first,
there's nothing to see, so we lean way over.

The tire's corner pocket is ablaze with scads
of tiny pearly white bodies who've eaten well.

We don't linger over dinner, our glasses going
quickly up to our mouths, coming down empty.

WINTER FLOUNDER

Usually dark green on its upper side,
but turns over for a sweet, reddish
brown surface, with small dark spots.
Skirts the north Atlantic coast from
Georgia to Labrador, collecting thick
in the estuaries and bays, and can go
from surface to seventy fathoms just
like that; for the mud it prefers, or
sand and gravel we'd just kick away.

Something remarkable happens when
its larvae metamorphose: the left eye
moves over to the right side of the head
and starts to grin. There's no more work
to be done, so it just settles back to be
standard flounder, which would rather
die of embarrassment than be caught.

But it is, alas, more often than not,
in winter; usually by poor devils who
don't even know its name, or how to
fish it. They beg me for help cleaning
this one, and I suppose I'll wind up
cooking it too, so at least they will
remember filling their empty bellies.
Smell this! I lift the lid; there's that
eye, moving back to the other side.

QUARTER HORSE CURSE

Imagine eating a banana and dying
on the spot. Well, they can, thanks

to a defective gene so they can't
metabolize potassium readily, a pity

says the rancher hosting me at his
spread. Of all I learn, this fact alone

knifes the heart, but at least unlike
another guest I did not unknowingly

hold out a banana to an unsuspecting
animal, which collapsed as only horses

can, its legs shooting way past akimbo,
breaking its neck as if cracking a whip.

I'm thinking of leaving early, but take
some hesitating steps toward Lone Star,

an apple in my trembling fingers. This'll
be okay to nibble, I whisper in his muscled

ear. Down comes his holy head, lips parted,
great buck teeth wielded as if the tiniest of

vises. I watch eagerly for a long time as
his jaws do their work, filling the air with

loud chatter, infinitely superior to me, never
mind the possibility of serious comparison.

CHRISTMAS DINNER

You're Charles Darwin, in Patagonia collecting specimens,
eager to come upon a pygmy rhea, so rare they seem mythic

to some, when it dawns on you, you've just been served one!
But only after smacking lips when the last morsel slides down

your throat, so here's what you do: run to the kitchen to look
for feathers and bones among the scarred scraps. The cook's

fond of talking: "Yes, we're happy the Lord's sent some back
from purgatory. We were about to throw out ancestral recipes,

twenty-two in all." "What do you imagine the Lord thinks of
you now?" Darwin whispered, his face turning pale; and saw

hilts of forks and knives in his mind's eye. "Good sir," the cook
said tauntingly, "Are you not well fed now?" Some minutes pass

till Darwin can take his leave, his hand opening and closing over
the little wishbone, seeming to apologize for some unknown crime.

ON PANKING

When the snow's too deep to dig a path
on go my best boots. I stamp along till it

hardens, crusting enough to walk barefoot,
something I do when I need toughening up,

right after another death in the family, say.
The cold shooting up through your bones

stops all the emotional tingling, your head
and eyes clear, although the owl flying by

shuffles your heart like a deck of cards.
The last tongues of ice have slipped back

into the mouth of the quarry, but it won't
freeze over. Everyone's praying to God to

turn back the temperature. "Unless you say
the One Above," Gramma stares, "You won't

be heard." I blink: ever try to look at a bright
light open-eyed? I know if I keep pounding

down my grief of the moment, the door will
open and she'll mouth what she always does:

"I don't understand, why are you hurrying
to die?" But I can't stop, not even when she

shouts, "Remember the last time you panked
a path so we could escape any emergency?"

She's rubbing a spot on the window free of
frost when I look back, wagging her finger

till I turn around for tea she's brewed all her life.
We sip through a lump of sugar between our teeth,

the nightmare of fleeing hobnail Cossack boots
alive, the roof above us aslant, taking on snow.

THESE ARGUMENTS

Some men have an idea they can love
other men. They introduced Plato to
Socrates at twenty; one was handsome,
the other good and hungry. A moment
of pure suspense: they passed urine
in the brush, scattered dogs, told
jokes, climbed the stairs for bed.

In their sleep they stopped short
of killing. Let's wade no deeper
in these arguments, they breathed.
In the morning they told each other
their dreams, ate good fish; what
do you mean, hatred? They yawned;

5 1/2 to 6 feet tall, strong enough to
handle ideas without throwing up,
but Plato's tongue went stiff while
Socrates kept his mouth stuffed, so
Plato might die safely. We imagine

we can see them in the square from
the window. But how is it we don't
know how to clear our heads of them?
Heat the oven; wake up naturally? Does
this come of our living separately, going
off to the desert to think about all we
have learned? To find a kind of answer?

BEAZLESTONE

The one in Dad's pocket; could make us sweat.
"Got it out of a deer's runnet," he said. "When
I went to dress it. Listen, when I'm long gone

and dead, water's over the dam, clouds are
fuming, get the hell out of here; and stop
killing more deer. Can you do that for me?
It's your mother who had a taste for venison."

When I cleaned out his workbench, there was
a pail filled with beazles. He'd been busier
dressing more deer than I ever counted or ate.

I did have one last thought before sweeping up:
How well he aimed, who left me his twelve-gauge.
I clean and oil it now and then, but with nothing
like the perfection he'd have demanded, his eyes

growing small, that whistle coming over his lips
when he'd bend down, pat his beagle's head. "Not
now, boy, not just now," he'd always say at last.

RABBIT DEW

Technically, the ground mist after a quick shower on a hot day.
Add some feeding rabbits you always trip over around here.

If I did something suspicious, Gramma would say I had a bit of it
around me. Like a halo, she'd wink, if I confessed to committing …

Farther behind, the memory of her cuts into a shaded wood. It's
cool but oh so close there, the path narrowing to gravel and sand.

Which is what it's like to have trouble remembering things you're
imperiled to forget—all that makes it to the brain cells a rabbit's

bloody paw it gnawed at in your trap. I confess it should have taken
me longer to recover, but now that I have, all that's left is the glimmer
of stumbling into something alive. If I'm to begin at the beginning.

V. ALMOST AN AFTERTHOUGHT

ON LOVE

But nothing has happened in the first
half hour. We go on with our quarrel,
catch up for a time with what is false;
by accident we drink a bottle, make
a pact to write things down next time.
We've been everywhere on threats:
a knock much louder than a signal;
kidneys barely willing, ankles good
and drunk. Should we volunteer for
the past, slink back out of town, Love?

Your friends hope so; they talk, keep
watch, but no one's been where we've
been: twice, slowly, then three times—
the Chinese might call this a love poem
making its way slowly up the Great Wall.

KNAUTSCHKE

—for Anette & Thomas

Obaysch, the first hippo to reach Europe
since Roman times, inspired the "Hippo Polka,"
which my parents helped keep alive in Milwaukee
at the Steuben Society Social till WWII ended,
and they learned of Knautschke, one of the few
survivors of the animals in Berlin's fabled zoo.

"At least God," my mother said, "has vouchsafed
him more life." I promised to pay respects when I
traveled to Germany in 1949 as an exchange student,
and took a cheap room near what was left of the zoo.
Every day for a week I sat on the bench, watching
Knautschke keep his act going for the pitiful few,
who took time off from surviving for a little stroll
past his sad island. He'd take an hour or so to nose
a large, scarred wooden block, which seemed fallen
from a bombed building, gingerly up out of the moat,
almost to the top of his compound, before nonchalantly
circling it, pausing to look us over, before he sent it
plunging back down into the muddy water, almost
as an afterthought and an old woman hollered out,
"That's an animal who'd find God if He existed."

BLACKNOSE SHARK

When his family moved to the suburbs,
he was suddenly only one of two Jews

at school. With that broken nose of his,
his obvious name, it wasn't long till he

was called Flat Nose Kike; and the taunts
too numerous to beat back. So I understand,

when Biology 1 field-tripped to the aquarium,
his trance when he came across it in the corner

of its tank. The plaque said something about
its peculiarly long snout, jagged teeth that are

deeply notched, an odd, second dorsal fin:
often found in the stomach of other sharks.

That night, Jake started drawing it over and
over, begging his mother to sew a patch of

the fish's profile high up on his coat's sleeve.
Perhaps you can guess the rest—all the kids

wanted in on the club. At the first meeting,
at the end of the longest pier into the lake, he

handed out poles: First one's an FNK, he winked.

THE TANKS

Very early in bed,
German hands are
like thistles, prick
downward to pull
up what
they most want.

The leaves harden
to hair; negative light
sliding through lice
in the guards' beards.

Under the angels
like Rilke's, the tanks
fan out, enter the field
from the holy rear.

NEAR DACHAU

A yard away I remove my cap,
what could I have done? I try
not to raise my voice, but I
need to talk loud: why did you

marry a Jew and insist on staying
behind, as if that was an answer?
(While Uncle fled with the children
across the poor channel.) Remember

the doctor who counted the lumps
on your breasts, advised surgery,
bowed, and wished you *Gute Nacht*?
I looked him up between thumb and

index finger, demanded an account
of the chemistry of your blood. You
look better now, as I bear down on
my knees, bring you these lilies,

a tedious task for a man with less
to do now than before the war. Allies
came too late; did not interrupt that
last shower, but did take off helmets

as they passed feverishly by, spat
between their legs, the enormous
ditches still smoldering on the far
side of the rusting barbed wire.

MORE ON LYING

Since no one can say when he doesn't,
he talks himself into lying all the time;
and it has nothing to do with the truth.
Then, in spring, he falls ill. Lymphoma.
Reads some books, takes a few pills,
goes to a party if you can believe it; has
the best conversation he's ever had: with
a German writer who raises her leg when
he shakes her hand, or looks right through
him; he can't quite be certain. Then he sees
a French film of a German camp, in soft,
grainy colors; slow pans along barbed wire.
When the people in front of him whisper
the bones remind them of a Henry Moore,
he runs up the aisle, screaming. If he finds
his way home, he can't play the piano for her,
who's somehow down the basement now,
filling the washer, raising the ironing board.

An animal runs away fast; the stillest water
in the painting's a large section in the center.
He stands in front of it a long time, forgets
how much the depth changes with the light.
Where is Regensburg? The writer lives there.
Will she die? Maybe he hasn't told the truth
since Regensburg, doesn't realize the depth
has changed. Truth seems out of the question,
now: if he does tell it, he works it steady and
fast across the surface, till she comes up for
air or he goes down. The sky's nightmarish.

EINSTEIN IN BERLIN

>   —for RR & GN

"If the stomach of Germany weren't empty,
Hitler wouldn't be where he is," he was careful

to murmur under his breath, walking later and
later at night, hands on his back, occasionally

stooping to tie a shoe, which came undone on
its own, beyond his comprehension; he allowed

as how it never happened when he'd have too
much to drink, after holding his tongue at recent

meetings of physicists now sporting Nazi armbands.
But nothing else made much sense at the time either,

till he finally up and left, past soldiers falling down
to rest after drilling in steamy fields out the train's

filthy windows. All this might have ended in a different
way, had something else not happened in German minds.

SOMEWHERE NEAR MINSK

The wound seems like just a scratch,
but the blood comes as if poured from
a whiskey bottle. There are buttons
in it and a dead butterfly. Before I

die, I fall on my face like Gandhi,
sprinkle a little earth on soft palms
and work at being shy. What is your
blood type? the medic yells, Can you

read and write? This is a hot place for
a hospital. The doctor's muddy boots
are stuffed with flames. He gives me
plasma with a flourish, the colonist

type from fertile territories of Red
Cross America; the broad oak of
truckers' arms, jolting through as
over churned roads. I can sense

the strength of generations in it, am
so moved I write my hometown paper:
Dear Folks, here's hoping. A decent
statue and all that … Commissioned

and amortized. Start moving my kids'
arms to embrace it, but only if they are
so inclined; and may my unborn child
guard its shattered head between his legs.

In a niche the shell has reached, eyes
bare statuesque veins, while the ruins
of the western body hide inside muddy
huts, squatting on a narrow hill in Russia.

HONORABLE INTENTIONS

The bare level of our honorable intentions;
wires curling between the fingers, faces
hollow but smiling. It's a kind of pure duty,
gathering soldiers together for the mission:
a single village, a simple order to the platoon.

The Lt. tells the Sgt. to move in, the sewing
class begins to weep. This conduct is wrong!
So long to the needle-point faces; we all feel
lost, fray, fall back on accents, till the 'copter
relents. Low sun in a rising sky; few clouds.

Pointless accidents are severe expressions of
intoxicated emptiness. The lid drops on arms
turning toward heads; emotion down the line;
one by one; a morning buzzing with tiny flies.

BUT THAT THE WICKED TURN
FROM EVIL WAYS AND LIVE

Altogether a pleasant spot, with the usual
touch of melancholy. The second bridge,
of stone, farther out, on the highway; but
we knew nothing of each other really.
So is it right and proper to go on like that?
Some can hardly understand the quandary.

The sun's risen, what phenomenal confusion!
A long way from here, closer to Eden, wishes
will amount to nothing. But we don't know how
to get there. Our faces flushed, we start selling
off the furniture, next our belongings, right down
to the silk in the boxes. It would have been just
the same if there were no God, whom we watch
for, expect to return on foot, indignant, to claim
his imperfect children. But. And. But. And …

SHADOW

—for Shirley

The one cast across the donkey's back
by Christ's cross. Watching, a man caught
in the throng might have easily lost his meal,
before stumbling back up his steps to shout
the news to his wife, who'd fumble for her
thimble, the wax hardening to her imprint
when she scratched a note to her sister.

They weren't water drinkers, so she ran
for the wine but it tasted wrong, their cups
tipping in their hands, the wine staining
the floorboards, on its way out to the Via
Dolorosa and now, two millennia removed,
we're hunched in their doorway, looking
down at the blood leaking under the jamb.
Our guide says something in Arabic before
motioning us to kneel. We don't remember
what, and may not have even heard a word.

ANADROMOUS

Meaning fish, which normally live in the sea,
but run up into fresh water rivers and streams
to spawn, while other creatures, going the other

way to salt water, like eels, we call catadromous.
Open that lid, and you'll find both in my fishtrap.
Go ahead, you'd do me a favor, maybe strip me

from this spot altogether, where my luck's a magnet
for opposites. The natives are after one or the other,
catching both's a ticket to doom, they will tell you.

Twenty bucks apiece, I sing out, but everyone just cuts
way around me, wants nothing to do with someone
who can't make up his mind, they mutter. I'm not

such an ass, I want to say, my method's thought out
well beforehand. I can't help it if ... All this wouldn't
matter if we lived in less barbarous times, I console

myself now. But then there's this awful reminiscence:
it was still damn dark when I woke up, so of course
I baited the hooks wrong, while I was still living.

MOONLIGHT'S

Bad for you if you're a tiny critter
whose predators can spot you nights,

smashing twigs that come between,
their teeth itching to kiss your neck.

They've no business there, you might
have thought if you can think at all,

following them with your eyes, the way
my uncle's eyes followed the torpedo

surging along the moonlit alley between
the Japanese sub and his ship, his chest

rattling, his lips freezing till all was quiet
as the fish missed, only the lapping waves

and someone aft playing the harmonica in
a gloomy frame of mind. When my uncle

taught me how to drive right after the war,
in his new coupe bought with his severance

pay, he said before he let me turn the key:
Always remember, cars are mean killers.

We were out under some moon, the light
of those slain vanished from our eyes.

HOOKED DEEP

Do this to a fish and it won't fight
with all its might. Do this to a bass
guarding its nest—the brackish water

was no excuse: my expensive shades
see ten feet down through most anything—
it'll sicken you so much you might give up

fishing altogether, as I have since the three
of us sibs, the envy of all our friends, would
make time to go fishing twice a year on our

spiffy Ranger, were killing them that cloudy
day when we had other things we could have
done together, if I'd only proposed something.

The oldest by years—"I could only handle one
of you at a time," Mom would say not jokingly—
I blame myself for sitting on my little throne

so long till I lost it, screamed things I'm still
sorry for … Oh, they still go fishing together,
chiseling some time out of separate lives,

we still make nice if we turn up in the same
quadrant, but I try not to trouble them with
details of my own nothingness now. I do go

out nights on a little raft on the local reservoir,
keep casting till my wrist aches, telling myself
it's good aerobic exercise, but there's no hook

on the wooden plug at line's end, and I'm more and more careless about "putting it in the ring," which pros do so automatically, as if blind.

SHOES

The donkey-skinned pair God ordered
Moses to remove before treading holy soil.

Did he sit down to do so, or perhaps
lean on his staff, bend over unsteadily

to pull them off, the sun's rays already
reaching him from below the horizon,

his eyes closing like fists, his hair caked
with mud? Was he dying to know how long

he'd been dying, but afraid to ask? If he'd
laughed to lighten the moment, he'd have

been alone with his laughter, heading toward
a grave full of slush and snow—I read it could

have been snowing! At this time in my own
little life, busy getting older, I'm willing to

accept anything too, and so on and so forth.

ADMITTING WE WERE BORN

When will you tire
of sitting next to doors,
feeding animals and children,
even in the dark ages
women kept guard at night,
the sky rushed back as if
it had forgotten something
and the sun became the number
one fuel, there one moment
and the next, tapping its head
till it grew light and we finally
undressed, turned sleeves inside
out, the light so deep we watched
it, settled back and just watched,
we're watching it now but if we
turn around in what is called
the magic art of looking back,
men go to women, water to wells.

THANK THE ONE ABOVE

i
Nominal Jews like me, never past secular at best,
love Catholics, Catholic women in particular,
Christmas trees too (I trim a pretty nifty one), &
pork of course, among countless other markers.

We donate regularly to Catholic Charities (known
to keep administrative costs to a minimum). Let me
also note, I leapt to renew *Commonweal* in my name
when my wife's subscription lapsed, look forward

to cooking for her new priest when it's time to have
him over. Father Frank, now retired, didn't care what
the menu was, as long as we had Boodles gin on hand,
though he waved aside my pitiful efforts to shake him

a proper martini, just poured an overflowing jigger down
some ice cubes and never mind the vermouth. "How bout
them apples?" he winked, which has since become my
go-to mantra for just-do-it situations. Now that I know

the new priest not only condones my recent decision to
donate my body to the local med school, but adds the act's
heartily endorsed by The Church, for its support-of-life
dimensions, I'm thinking of looking into RCIA sessions.

I don't dare mention my firm intention in public anymore,
after my old pal blanched, way too upset: "No thanks for
guaranteeing I see you as a cadaver from now on, damn
you …" And my wife, who'd been leaning toward gifting

her remains too, has enjoined me from blabbing it or else,
especially not at the P.O., where I do time every day, love
mentioning to anyone in line I ask for my own window at
Christmas but never seem to get it. As for blabbing, I admit

I told my doctor-daughter, whose own Anatomy 101 cadaver
I once got to meet, because I wanted her approval most of all;
been turning to her more & more, not just for an emergency
prescription when I wake up scared & sweating these darker

nights. She's careful as an angler releasing an undersize trout,
so I get to swim back into all my notions of what it might be
like to kneel at the altar, close eyes, stick out my tongue while
whatever's left of the Jew in me, full of presentiments, waits

for some word from The One Above. Gramma said NEVER
EVER say the G-word unless you're willing never to sleep
in the same bed again, face an empty room, save for your old
rabbi behind his enormous desk, pulling his beard out when

you wailed, But I don't want to read or write right to left, I
only stalked Harlene Harberg home from Hebrew School to
see if she was going to survive the after-effects of her beauty
& fall in love with me before the pendulum fell off the clock.

ii

Been lately hard to resist the temptation to take Communion,
especially for the cook in me who's got to have a taste before
dishing anything out to others. When my dying mother stuck
her tongue out for a bit of macaroni & cheese—I was feeding

her at The Jewish Home for the Aged—little white spots made
me drop the spoon. "Go, and don't come back till you've gotten
past revulsion," she whispered, "I'll be here till I'm no longer
wanted." You could see in her face she was a great Latinist

in high school, said she'd have married Cicero if he'd only
stuck around. I'm looking at her old highschool report cards
now, a string of 99s for 8 semesters of Latin, high marks too
for math—no wonder she loved helping me with algebra -

but pretty average grades in everything else, especially typing,
which she said was worth skipping class to sunburn at the beach.
Should have asked her more about her own religious leanings,
because of all the Garbers she seemed the most spiritual, flew

at the rabbi who had it in for me, seized him by the sleeve:
"As far as I can judge," she raised her voice, "My son is impulsive
but not argumentative." "So?" Is all he said in an agitated voice,
& that did it, Saturdays from then on free for sandlot football, till

I broke my nose and needed more than just sulfa, the very first
lot to be used by the general public near war's end. Dr. Schwartz,
an old Navy man, tapped connections to get me enough to not die.
His good Catholic wife came by daily, during her hospital ministry,

and politely asked if she could pray over me, let me fondle her rosary.
The next day she brought me my very own, said to work the beads
as if making a nice necklace for my mother for Christmas. She left
me singing Fall On Your Knees, O Hear the Angel Voices, O Christ

something or other. I slipped back under again, seized by the hand in a dream. Christ opened it, put something in, closed it again. "What's the matter with you," my mother said, when I woke up in a sick-sweat. I implored her to give me time to think things over, "Just a little time!"

iii

Ever since, that moment's bought me more & more time to do nothing but while away more time. My mother lit another cigarette, and let me blow out the match. She's been long gone, she who could solve painful equations of my relationships, mostly by sitting silently by, sipping her

Blatz, while I drew little Vs. "Birds flocking," I said when the page was full, "toward God." "Here, take a little more tapioca," she cooed, my favorite comfort food. "How can he stomach those little fish eyes," my father said when he came home from "making a living so you'll

have it better than us." He'd changed his name from Felix-Immanuel, so his customers wouldn't know you-know-what. More than once I heard him just swallow hard when guys said Kike and the like. But for him I'd not have learned how to catch muskys, filet them just right

for Gramma's gefilte fish. Both of us stopped short of total indifference to one another. He would of course understand, if mistakenly, why I'd go Catholic at this time in my life, curse everyone else for making it inevitable, trudge off into the woods to shoot another deer to dress, but

stamp back clenching fists if he missed his shot. When he lay dying, refusing to rehab a broken hip, I tried cursing him back, hoping his bile would boil up again; caught myself in shameful thoughts, how do you know reformation will set in? "I'll miss you some," is all he said, closed one eye and died. I sat down on his bed as if everything were all right; "He won't do it again," ringing in my ears, when mother once begged him—"for Christ's sake"—not to take his belt to me. I'd been building Japanese Zeros on his workbench without permission,

stupidly left a mess behind, his anger compounded: I loved Zeros for their markings, even though they were shooting at my uncle off to war, which Dad just missed, so that must have had something to do with it. Huddling around the Kaltenborn news at supper, when it looked like

we might lose in the early going, we all Oyed in chorus, and I crossed myself, learned from Georgie Karji on the corner, so fast no one noticed. I'd better take another Ambien now, got to get some sleep so I won't bite my cheek till it bleeds, have come close to buying one of those restraining

bits to stop the gnashing. If you stood beside my bed, looked into my face, you'd call 911. And as for being a really good prospect for converting, I feel naked as a slave praising the Lord. Afraid of the next cloudburst. Not how one should live, unless forming an army and training them to die. But don't hurry.

High time now to bury the indulgencies. First take scissors and cut them up, then collage them for a target behind the bar in the basement. New Year's down there, with friends and family droning in and out, consuming vats of boiled shrimp, washing them down with Bloody Marys. I'd sharpen darts on

Dad's old lathe till he banged me on the back, snatched them away. "Here, let me show you how to hunt, Mr. Know-It-All." Never saw so many Bulls-Eyes in my stupid life! Which blurt got me a pat on the head, a faint sign in Dad's face I might just amount to something after all. I must leave you now,

more excitement's bad for the heart, I've heard. Have to think about supper,
consolation in the bracing Catholic company of my wife, more and more
the reason life's easier. Though she seldom agrees with me, it's a good thing
she's willing to taste if not eat all of what I arrange as artistically as I can on

the stoneware we've yet to wear down to its elements. The candle lit, the dark
coming down, we can just make out the last of the birds at the feeder, always
a female cardinal and a downy male woodpecker hanging upside down from
the suet staked on top, no more cross-bills to make their quieter life miserable.

Raising our glasses, we say a little prayer I learned in Germany once, from
the old Catholic innkeeper, when away so long I got so homesick if I hadn't
bailed out of the translation project, and hightailed it back to Ohio, who knows
what … "Bread from wheat, wheat from light, light from the sight of God."

ON THE EVE OF THE END

We shall see it all, perhaps due to the wine.
The lamp's dimming, the furniture's rather
poor, but we've found out all we've wished
to know. The voice in our head: "Departure
ahead!" We start smiling more gently, not
only because the terror's starting to melt
away and the crops have stopped growing.

Squeezing ourselves through the opening
in the middle distance, "Lord have mercy!"
slipping off our tongue, there's little time
left to be heard. When one of us starts to
yawn it's catching. No need for a sleeping
pill now, though a sleeping mask might help.
Quite so, our guide says, his feet sticking

to the snow in the field. "All one has to do,"
he says when we help him to his feet, "is…
But the wind's howling now, we can't hear
a syllable. No one told us anything about
this before we started out. When we're out
of sight, you may go back to your reading,
but expect a bright light, your eyes to blink.

www.ingramcontent.com/pod-product-compliance
Lightning Source LLC
Chambersburg PA
CBHW021015090426
42738CB00007B/798